Heirloom
Smocking

Heirloom Smocking

Fiona J. Roediger

Kangaroo Press

Acknowledgments

Putting together a book like this is an awesome task, and cannot be undertaken without the love and support of many special people. So for their help, support, encouragement and love I give my sincere thanks to:

- Jill Parker and her fabulous staff at 'The Studio', Tony Carey Photographers of Port Lincoln. Thank you for your encouragement. Once again your expertise was outstanding.
- Ruth Dennis, 'Kurrabi Lodge,' Koppio, South Australia. A huge thank you for your enthusiasm and your wonderful garden.
- Barb Millard, Koppio National Trust Museum, for sweeping away all the cobwebs.
- Maxine and Bob McRostie, for the use of your front verandah.
- Suzanne Lawrie, 'Tumby Cottage Crafts', Tumby Bay, for the beautiful wool embroidered bear.
- Lorraine Brown and Bev Roediger, for organising the picnic lunch, keeping me sane, and just coping with the chaos.
- Garths Shoe and Sports Store, Tumby Bay, for the loan of quite a few pairs of shoes.

- Vanessa Brooks, Rebecca (Little Beck) Lovegrove, Kelly Roediger, Ghia Spangenberg, Blaise Baldissera, Somma Baldissera, Lana Roediger, Jae Fitzgerald, Melinda Baldissera, Nadia Baldissera, Hannah Pfitzner, Emilie Fauser and Callen Hammond: thirteen delightful and wonderful models who did their job to perfection.
- Kerry Spangenberg, Karen Baldissera, Marlene Roediger, Judy Baldissera, Sue Pfitzner, Annette Hammond and Sarah Fauser, all models' mums. Thank you all for holding my hand all day.
- Pamela Wilkins and Helen Colman, two very generous friends whose continued support and encouragement is very much appreciated.
- My mum, who made me promise to do this again.
- And last but by no means least my husband Ken, who once again put up with it all. I thank you for your support, encouragement and love.

—Fiona

First published in 1995 by Kangaroo Press Pty Ltd
3 Whitehall Road Kenthurst NSW 2156 Australia
PO Box 6125 Dural Delivery Centre NSW 2158
Printed in Hong Kong through Colorcraft Ltd

ISBN 086417 688 0

Contents

Introduction

The art of smocking, a classic embroidery technique which allows a creative use of individual expression with both colour and design, is far simpler than it appears.

Smocking was originally devised in the rural areas of England, when protective smocks were worn. Smocking the front and back of a garment gave it extra fullness as well as adding extra warmth. These garments also had to be hard-wearing, practical and comfortable.

Fortunately, what was once just practical became so ornamental and pretty that smocking became a fashion feature which remains very popular today, particularly on babies' and children's clothes.

Once you have the feel for a few favourite stitches, you can be a little more adventurous, adding roses, ribbons and bows to turn an ordinary outfit into something special.

Materials and equipment

Fabric

We all want our finished garments to be worn and much loved by their wearers. When selecting fabric, remember not only colour, washability and texture, but the wearer's personality.

If you are a beginner choose simple open prints with one solid main colour, or a plain fabric. It is much easier to follow a smocking design on such a fabric. Cotton blend fabrics give the best results, as they tend to keep their shape better than other fabrics and wash well. Try crushing a piece of fabric in your hand before you buy it—if it creases very easily it will need a fair amount of ironing.

Choose the fabric and garment design to suit the wearer; a drop-waisted dress looks good on a taller or slimmer girl, but it does not suit a smaller child.

Once a piece of fabric is smocked it is reduced to one-third of its original width, so if your finished article needs to be 20 cm wide you will need a 60 cm width of fabric after selvages have been removed.

Needles

Select a needle that will push through your fabric with ease, with an eye large enough for easy threading. A No. 7 or No. 8 crewel is usually suitable. Keep a spare needle in your handbag to try in the fabrics you are considering buying; that way you can buy extra needles to suit a particular fabric if necessary.

Thread

Embroidery threads are available in a wide variety of colours and types, but I find I use DMC No. 8 Perle Coton most of the time. It comes in a ball and doesn't become twisted and knotted like most of the stranded cottons. It keeps very tidy, and there is no wastage from throwing away unwanted strands. If you prefer to use stranded cotton, however, use three strands of thread. As most stranded cottons have more than the three strands required they will have to be divided.

If you are smocking a child's dress from selvage to selvage, you will need to work with a one-metre length of thread. This will allow you to work across the pleated fabric without running out of thread, thus avoiding knots on the inside which tend to look untidy.

When selecting thread for a smocking project choose a shade darker than your fabric rather than lighter—a darker shade will stand out more. Always write down the number and colour of the thread that you have selected. I keep a special notebook with a page for each project I do; I attach to the page a piece of the fabric and small lengths of each thread I have used, identified by the type and colour number. This helps later on with colour coordination. I find this book invaluable when I buy thread, as there are always so many colours to choose from.

A design can change simply by changing the colour of the thread; the whole effect can be altered this way, which makes smocking interesting. It is really up to your own imagination. You will be amazed at how creative you can be—but be warned, fabric and craft shops may become irresistible!

Added touches

To add a professional look when I am attaching smocking or inserting it into a garment, I use satin piping (which can be bought from most haberdashery stores) or lace. This also helps to stabilise the pleats. Satin piping highlights the smocked work (if you spend all that time on smocking, you want to make sure people notice your lovely needlework!) and is not particularly expensive. Adding embroidered roses around collars and cuffs or around necklines looks pretty and can really dress up a garment. If it suits the particular garment, wide satin ribbons sewn into the side seams, to be tied into bows, can add extra sparkle. The embroidered cotton collars available at most haberdashery shops suit some fabrics better. You will be surprised how many simple, attractive ideas for finishing touches you will find when you look around. Experiment with your own special skills as well—you might surprise yourself with how original and artistic you can be.

General rules for smocking

1. All stitches in this book are worked from left to right.
2. For upward stitches the thread is kept below the needle.
3. For downward stitches the thread is kept above the needle.
4. For cable stitches the thread may be either above or below the needle, depending on which direction the next stitch takes.
5. After making each stitch give the thread a gentle tug to keep the tension even and give consistency to the stitches.
6. If the thread frays or becomes difficult to work with, tie it off and begin with a new thread.
7. If you need to start a new thread halfway through a row, bring the needle up next to the stitch just completed and push it through the pleat on the left (stitch just completed).
8. Do not cut a panel of smocking without machine stitching the line of the cut first. If you need to cut out armholes, mark where they need to go and then sew two or three lines of straight stitch with your sewing maching. Smocking cut without doing this will all come undone like knitting.
9. Use the gathering threads as guidelines to keep your smocking stitches straight.
10. Spend a little time when you start, checking the first row of stitches for mistakes.
11. Keep your needle horizontal as you work, parallel to the gathering thread.

Starting and finishing

To start a row

To start a row, thread the needle and knot one end of the embroidery thread. Working from left to right, count three pleats across, and bring your needle from the back, between the third and fourth pleats, through to the right side. Now insert your needle into the third pleat. As you work each pleat pick up half the depth of the pleat. Your needle will be inserted from the right side of each pleat through to the left side (a form of back stitching). The needle is held horizontal, parallel to the gathering thread. Finish three pleats in from the other side also; this gives enough fabric for a flat surface for a seam.

To finish a row

To end a row, try to finish with a cable stitch if possible. Insert the needle into the valley between the last two pleats, taking it through to the back of the work. Pick up a little of the pleat and make a loop, pass the needle through the loop to make a tiny knot. Do this two or three times to make it secure.

Holding rows

When working smocking the first row and the last row of gathering are not smocked—these two rows are called holding rows. These rows stabilise the pleats and keep them even, making the smocking easier to manage.

Stitches

Outline stitch

This is a very simple stitch to do, as the thread is always kept *above* the needle. Keeping the needle level with the gathering thread, pick up the first pleat ready for stitching—remembering to keep the thread above the needle. Use your thumb to help keep it there. Now continue to pick up each pleat till the end of the row.

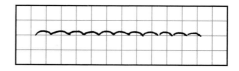

Diagram 1   Outline stitch

Stem stitch

This is the same stitch as the outline stitch, only this time the thread is *below* the needle. Again, use your thumb to help keep the thread in place.

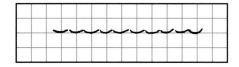

Diagram 2 Stem stitch

Wheat stitch

Wheat stitch combines outline stitch and stem stitch, worked on the same line with the outline stitch above the gathering thread and the stem stitch directly below the gathering thread. This forms an 'ear of wheat' effect. This combined stitch, which is very effective and really does look like wheat, works well on plain fabrics and fabrics with a simple pattern.

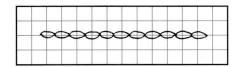

Diagram 3 Wheat stitch

Cable stitch

Cable stitch is the foundation for most smocking stitches. In cable stitch the thread is alternately above and below the needle. The needle never changes position, only the thread. Remember to keep the needle parallel to the gathering thread.

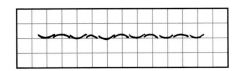

Diagram 4 Cable stitch

For a *bottom* or *under cable* the thread is below/under the needle.

For an *above* or *top cable* the thread is above/over the needle.

These are two of the most important rules for smocking.
Cable stitch is a good stitch for backsmocking.

Double cable stitch

Work one row of cable across the pleats, alternating the thread above and below the needle. Start with an under cable. Now work another row of cable directly underneath the first row, so that the stitches touch each other. Start with an over cable.

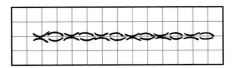

Diagram 5 Double cable stitch

Cable flowers

Work three cables (under-over-under), then directly below work another three cables (over-under-over). This looks lovely as a fill-in for diamonds.

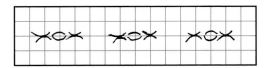

Diagram 6 Cable flowers

Alternating cable stitch

Alternating cable stitch is lovely when done in two colours. It is a little difficult to do at first, but the end result is worth it.
Starting with a bottom cable, work one row of cable stitches—this is our base row. Now start a new row directly below the first row of

stitches. Starting with a top cable, work three cables to the third cable (insert your needle diagonally from the right side of the pleat under the row above, pointing it upwards, and bring it out on the left side of the same pleat). Now do the next three cables *above* the base row. Before completing the third pleat insert the needle diagonally downward to come out underneath the first row of cable stitches.

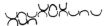

Now you are ready to do the next three-cable sequence. This may seem a little hard at first, but persevere with it—in the end you will be glad that you did.

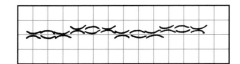

Diagram 7   Alternating cable stitch

Trellis stitches

With this stitch you work up and down between the gathering threads. It is often referred to as zig-zag stitch.

All trellises start and finish with a cable stitch.

It is most important to remember:

- When going *up* the thread is *below* the needle.
- When going *down* the thread is *above* the needle.
- For *bottom cables* the thread is *below* the needle.
- For *top cables* the thread is *above* the needle.

Whether going up or down the needle is still held horizontally and inserted into each pleat horizontal to the gathering thread, pointing back to the beginning of the work.

A cable stitch is used at the top and bottom of each zig-zag, and determines the direction of the next stitch.

A mistake is very easy to undo—just unthread the needle and gently push the eye under the thread to make it come out.

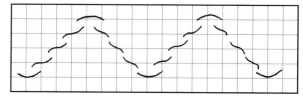

Diagram 8   Three-step trellis stitch

Trellis stitches are worked in 'steps' of 2, 3, 4 or more. The number of steps indicates how many stitches there are between the top and bottom cables. Decide before you start how many steps are required. If it's three steps, then space them at the one-quarter, one-half and three-quarter marks between the rows.

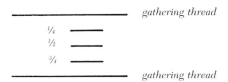

Start as you normally would, picking up the first pleat between halfway and the bottom gathering thread, picking up the next pleat at the halfway mark, then picking up the next pleat between the halfway mark and the top gathering thread. Pick up the fourth pleat and do a top cable above the line. Remember to change thread position—thread above the needle for a top cable.

As you move on to the next pleat, pick it up between the top gathering thread and the halfway mark, then pick up the next pleat at the halfway mark, the next pleat between the halfway mark and the bottom gathering thread. When you have completed the third stitch, do a bottom cable, remembering to change thread position.

As you come down with the trellis stitch it helps to keep the needle level with the upward stitch at that same level. Use your needle eye to help put stitches in the correct position.

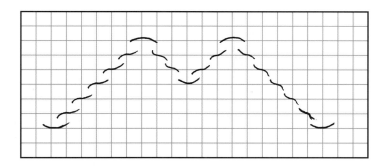

Diagram 9   Five-step trellis stitch

These are the instructions for a 3-step trellis; a 2-step, 4-step or 5-step trellis is worked in exactly the same way—the only difference is the number of steps. You can work another row of trellis stitches directly below the row just completed (see diagram 10), or reverse the trellis stitch to make a large diamond.

The possibilities with trellis stitch are endless—try a few ideas of your own. I like to do rows and rows of trellis stitch in different colours.

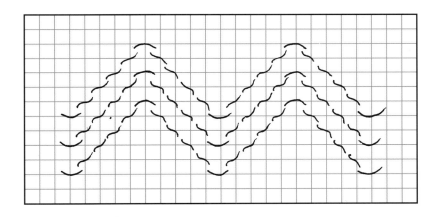

Diagram 10   Three rows of trellis stitches

Wave stitches

Wave stitch is one of my favourite stitches, and it combines well with other stitches. Wave stitch is worked between the rows of gathering threads.

Start in the usual way and do a bottom cable. With the thread below the needle follow the next pleat up to the gathering thread above, and pick it up. A top cable can now be done on the next pleat, remembering to change thread position. Follow the next pleat down to the bottom gathering thread and pick it up; now pick up the next pleat and do a cable for the bottom, remembering to change thread position.

Diagrams 11 and 12, showing wave stitch and baby wave stitch, are over the page.

thread above the needle

thread below the needle

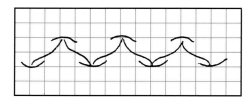

Diagram 11   Wave stitch

Cable and wave combinations

These stitches follow the same principle as the wave, the only difference being in the cables at the top and bottom. Try your own combinations of stitches and thread colours. You will be amazed at the number of choices you have—the huge variety of combinations.

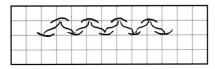

Diagram 12   Baby wave stitch

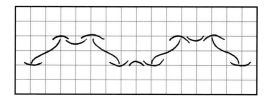

Diagram 13   Wave and 3-cable combination

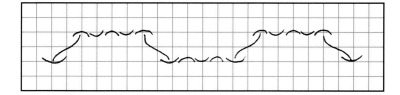

Diagram 14   Wave and 5-cable combination

These stitches are the basis for all the projects covered in this book.

Many books already available describe many more stitches, but these are the most commonly used. Happy smocking—it is never too late to learn!

Ribbon Weaving

Weaving ribbon through smocking adds a new dimension to smocked garments, creating something uniquely different. Use 3 mm double-sided satin ribbon threaded through a tapestry needle. To prevent the end of the ribbon slipping out of the eye, insert the point of the needle through the end of the ribbon, and pull the ribbon back through the eye.

The ribbon is woven through rows of baby waves, alternately under and over to form a zig-zag. At the top and bottom of each zig-zag fold the ribbon either upwards or downwards, depending on the direction it is to go. Use your left thumb to keep the ribbon in position. Straighten the ribbon before pulling it through the stitches.

Take extra care with this technique not to stretch the stitches.

The Patterns

Little Beck

A delicate dress of pale mauve para silk, based on the classic yoke style. Bullion roses embroidered on the smocking in the shape of a heart become the focal point. The collar is edged with delicate lace and narrow piping, and the same piping joins the front yoke to the front bodice. The sleeves feature traditional cuffs.

Instructions

Pleat 17 rows.

Row 1: Holding row—do not smock.
Row 2: Work a row of cable stitch.
Row 3: Work row 3 up to row 2 with a 4-step trellis.
Row 4: Work row 4 up to row 3 with a 4-step trellis.
Row 5: Work row 5 up to row 4 with a 4-step trellis.
Row 6: Work row 6 up to row 5 with a 4-step trellis.

The following rows of smocking are all worked with a 4-step trellis, forming the diamonds which will be embroidered with bullion roses.

Row 6: Work row 6 down to row 7 with a 4-step trellis.
Row 8: Work row 8 up to row 7, then down to row 9.
Row 10: Work row 10 up to row 9, then down to row 11.
Row 12: Work row 12 up to row 11, then down to row 13.
Row 13: Work row 13 down to row 14 with a 4-step trellis.
Row 14: Work row 14 down to row 15 with a 4-step trellis.
Row 15: Work row 15 down to row 16 with a 4-step trellis.

Instructions for the centre heart
Find the centre front of your garment and mark this point. The embroidered heart is four diamonds wide and three diamonds high. First mark and work the centre rose, then the two roses above left and those above right. Each rose is placed on a trellis junction. Back smock rows 6 to 12.

Each rose has a bullion stitch of 6 wraps for its centre; a second and third stitch positioned above and below the first one each have 8 wraps. Ten-wrap bullion stitches form the outside of the flower. Finish off each rose with a daisy-stitch leaf.

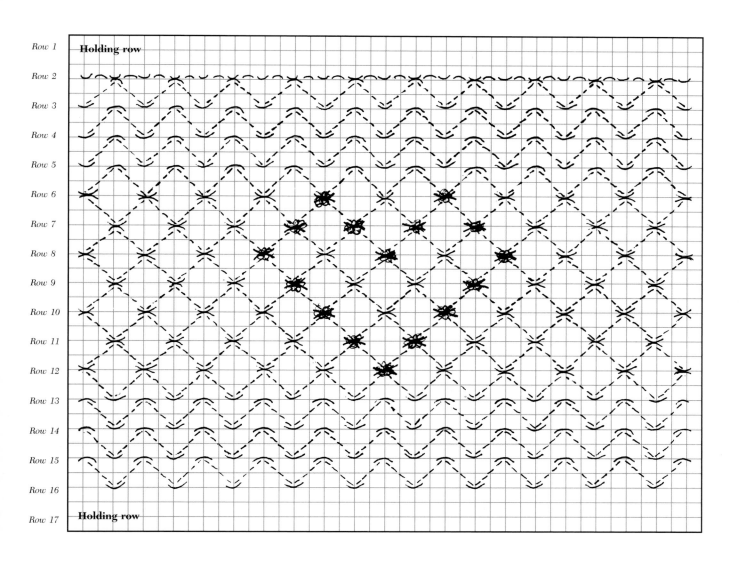

Little Beck

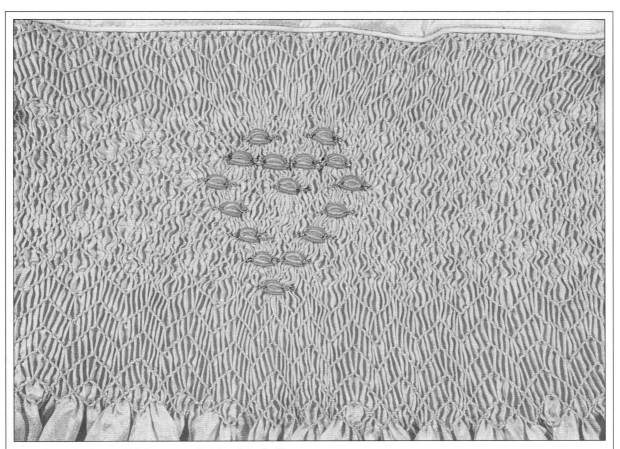

Detail of smocking with hearts embroidered in bullion roses

Detail of collar and cuff

Blaise

A pretty classic yoke dress to tempt the beginner. The smocking consists of trellis stitches, with 5 bullion roses in the centre to complement the design. Satin piping around the collar edge and satin piping and soft gathered lace at the top of the sleeve cuff contribute to the traditional look.

Instructions

Tip: Work all the full-space rows first, then work the half-space rows in between.

Pleat 14 full-space rows.

Row 2: Work cable stitches along the row.

Row 3: Work a 4-step trellis up to row 2, then down to row 4, forming a diamond.

Row 4: Work a 4-step trellis up to row 3, then down to row 5.

Rows 4½, 5, 5½, 6, 6½ are all worked with a 4-step trellis starting down.

Row 7 down to row 8, and *row 9* up to row 8 are both worked with a 4-step trellis, forming a diamond.

Rows 9½, 10, 10½, 11, 11½, 12, 12½ and 13 are all worked in a 4-step trellis starting in an upwards direction.

Five bullion roses are worked in the centre diamonds. Each rose has a 7-wrap stitch for the centre, and 9-wrap stitches around the outside.

Row 1   **Holding row**
Row 2
Row 3
Row 4
Row 5
Row 6
Row 7
Row 8
Row 9
Row 10
Row 11
Row 12
Row 13
Row 14   **Holding row**

Blaise

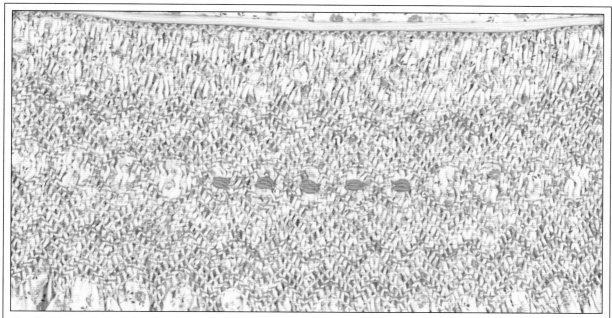

Detail of smocking and embroidered bullion roses

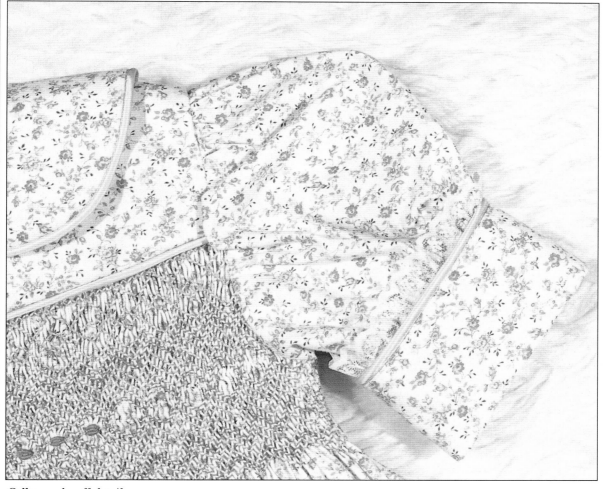

Collar and cuff details

Ghia

A delightful square-yoked classic dress with dropped back. Satin ribbon is woven through the smocking. The collar is piped with satin, and the sleeve cuffs are trimmed with piping and gathered lace.

Double-sided satin ribbon (3 mm wide) has been woven through rows 8 and 9, and again through rows 12 and 13. See instructions for weaving ribbon through smocking (page 14).

Instructions

Pleat 20 half-space rows (10 full-space).

Row 2: Row 2 is worked with a cable stitch across the row first; then work a three cable and baby wave down to row 3.
Rows 3 to 19 are all worked with a baby wave stitch.

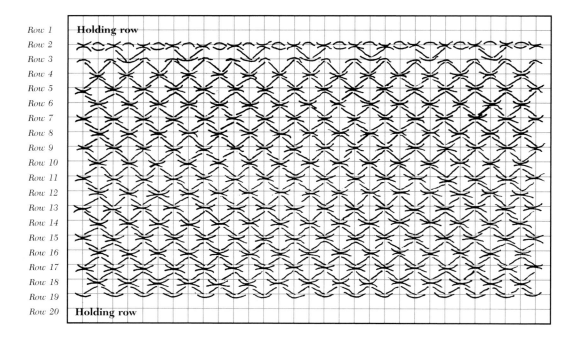

24

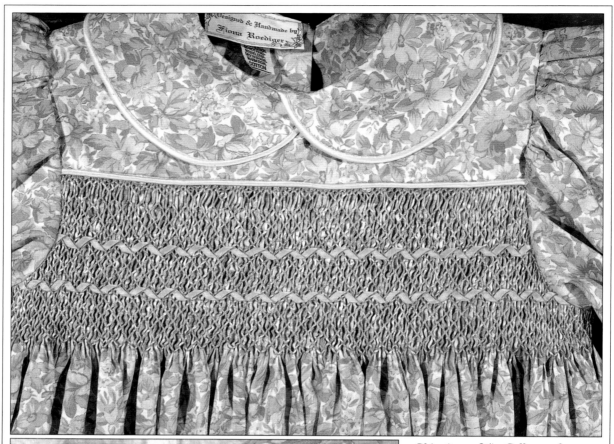

Ghia (page 24): Collar and smocking set off by satin piping

Ghia: Detail of sleeve trim

Hannah

A charming bishop-style baby dress smocked with trellis stitches to form a central row of hearts highlighted by embroidered roses.

Instructions

Pleat 11 half-space rows.

Row 2: Work a row of cable stitches.
Row 4: Work row 4 up to row 3 with a 2-step trellis.

Row 5: Work row 5 up to row 4 with a 2-step trellis.
Row 6: Work row 6 up to row 5 with a 2-step trellis, then work row 6 down to row 8 with a 5-step trellis.
Row 7: Work row 7 down to row 9 with a 5-step trellis.
Row 8: Work row 8 down to row 10 with a 5-step trellis.

If desired grub roses can be worked inside the heart shapes.

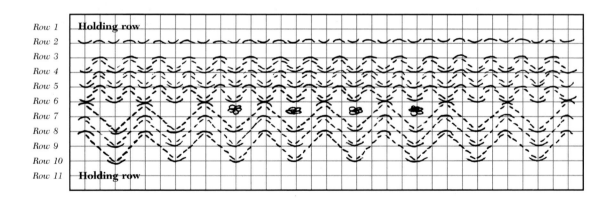

27

Hannah

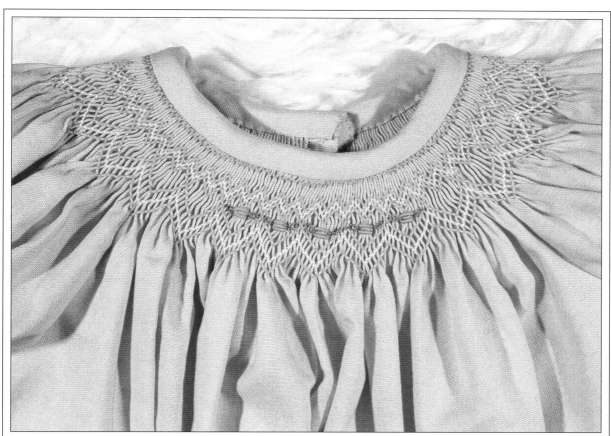

Detail of smocking around the neck of the bishop-style dress

Emilie

A bishop-style baby dress smocked with cables, baby waves and trellis stitches in a traditional floral fabric of soft pinks, mauves and muted green.

Instructions

Pleat 9 half-space rows.

Row 2: Work cable stitches across the row. Then directly below the cables work 3 cables, then a baby wave down to row 3, another 3 cables, and a baby wave back up to row 2. Repeat this pattern across the fabric.

Row 3: Work 3 cables, then a baby wave down to row 4, another 3 cables, and a baby wave back up to row 3.

Row 4: Work 3 cables, then a baby wave down to row 5, another 3 cables, and a baby wave back up to row 4.

Row 5: Work a row of cable stitches along the row. Then work a 4-step trellis down to row 7.

Row 6: Work a 4-step trellis down to row 8.

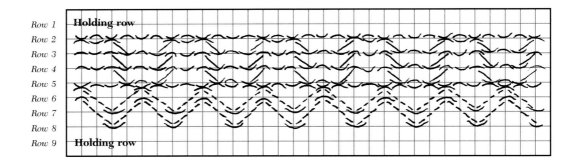

Emilie's dress is set off by a broderie anglaise trim on the sleeves

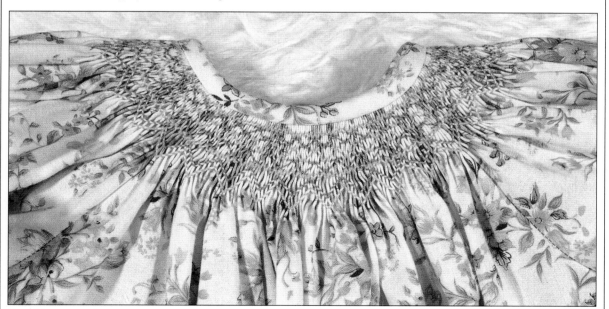

Smocking extends around the neckline

Kelly Belle

This classic yoked dress has a Victorian look.

Embroidered grub roses in the shape of hearts highlight the front bodice, and the contrast collar features self piping with chain stitch embroidery. The same contrast fabric is used for the trim attached at the front yoke and bodice, without piping cord, and the cuffs.

A 5.5 cm (2¼'') tuck is made 13 cm (5'') above the hem edge. The waist sashes are 12 cm (4¾'') wide with a pleat in the middle of each.

Instructions

Pleat 20 full-space rows.

Row 2: Work a straight cable along the whole row. Then directly beneath this row work a 3 cable, then a baby wave down to row 2½. Repeat this sequence across the row.
Row 3: Work with cable, then alternating cable stitches.
Row 5: Work a 4-step trellis up to row 4. With a contrast thread start at row 4 and work down to row 5 with a 4-step trellis, crossing over the previous row.

The following rows are all worked with a 4-step trellis using the main colour. This forms the diamonds onto which the three heart shapes are embroidered.

Row 5: Down to row 6.
Row 7: Up to row 6, and down to row 8.
Row 9: Up to row 8, and down to row 10.
Row 11: Up to row 10, and down to row 12.
Row 13: Up to row 12, and down to row 14.
Row 15: Up to row 14 and down to row 16.
Row 17: Up to row 16, and down to row 18.
Row 18: Work row 18 down to row 19, and row 19 up to row 18, crossing over.

The hearts

Each heart shape is 5 diamond points wide and 4 diamond points high. The pattern extends across 15 diamond points on the front yoke.

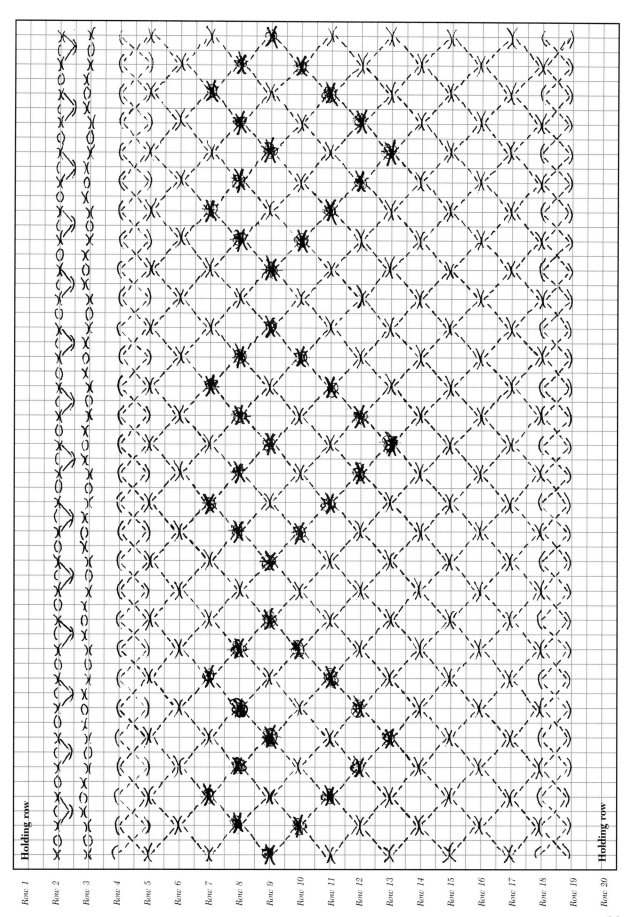

Row 1

Holding row

Row 2

Row 3

Row 4

Row 5

Row 6

Row 7

Row 8

Row 9

Row 10

Row 11

Row 12

Row 13

Row 14

Row 15

Row 16

Row 17

Row 18

Row 19

Row 20

Holding row

Kelly Belle

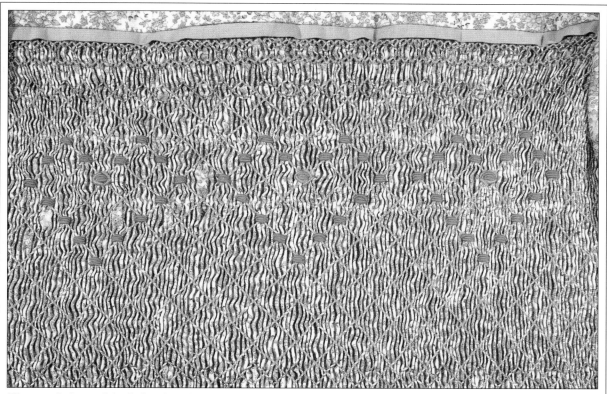

The smocked panel includes three hearts embroidered in grub roses

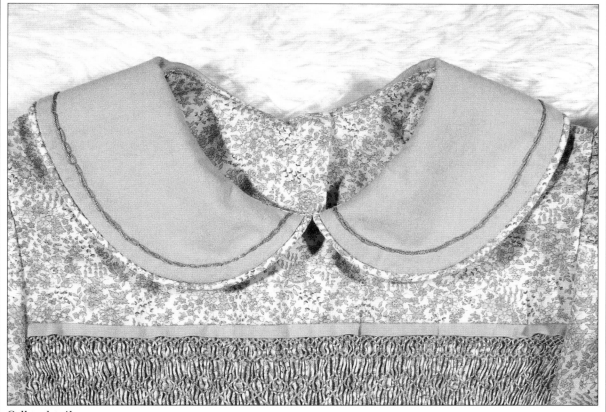

Collar detail

Autumn Frolic

A lavish use of trellis stitch combined with ribbon weaving creates a stunning look.

This dress has a double collar edged with satin piping. The under collar is in the same contrast fabric used for the sleeve cuffs and hem edge. Cotton broderie anglaise lace has been used to join the skirt and hem edges together.

Instructions

Pleat 21 rows.

Row 2: Work row 2 with a cable stitch along the row, then starting directly under the first cable stitch work a 3-cable and 1 baby wave down to row 2½.

Rows 4, 4½, 5 and 5½ are all worked as a 5-step trellis starting with an upward trellis.

Row 6: Work row 6 down to row 6½ with a baby wave.

Row 7: Work row 7 up to row 6½ with a baby wave, ensuring that the centre points meet.

Rows 9 up to 8, 9½ up to 8½, 10 up to 9, 10½ up to 9½, 11 up to 10, 11½ up to 10½, 12 up to 11, 12½ up to 11½, and 13 up to 12 are all worked as a 5-step trellis, starting with an upward trellis.

Row 14: Work row 14 down to row 14½ with a baby wave stitch.

Row 15: Work row 15 up to row 14½ with a baby wave stitch.

Rows 16½ up to row 15½, 17 up to 16, 17½ up to 16½, 18 up to 17, 18½ up to 17½, and 19 up to 18 are all worked as a 5-step trellis.

Row 19: Now work row 19 down to row 20 with a 5-step trellis.

Row 20: Work row 20 up to row 19 with a 5-step trellis.

Work full-space rows first, then work the half-space rows in between (this makes it easier to judge the correct distance between rows). Try using as many thread colours as possible for an interesting look.

Satin ribbon 3 mm wide has been woven through the baby wave stitches: row 6 down to 6½, and 7 up to 6½, and again at row 14 down to 14½ and 15 up to 14½.

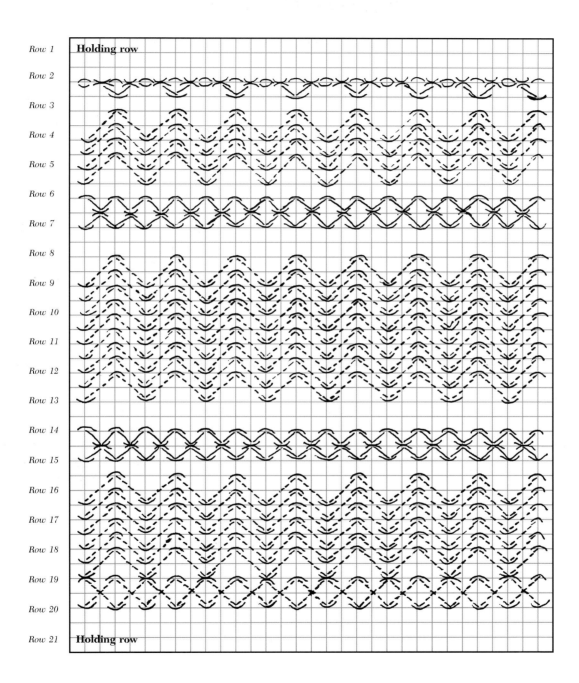

Autumn Frolic

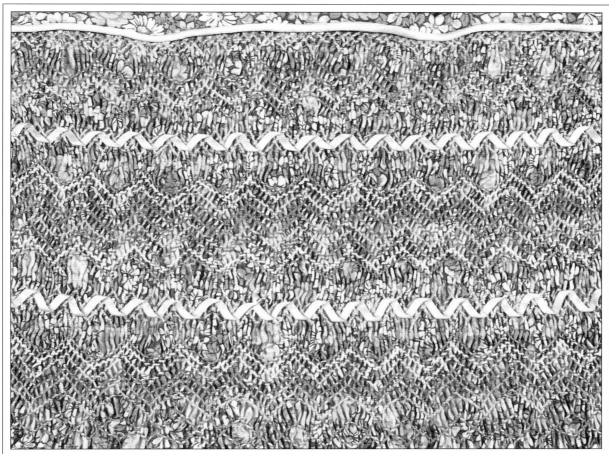

Smocked panel showing ribbon weaving

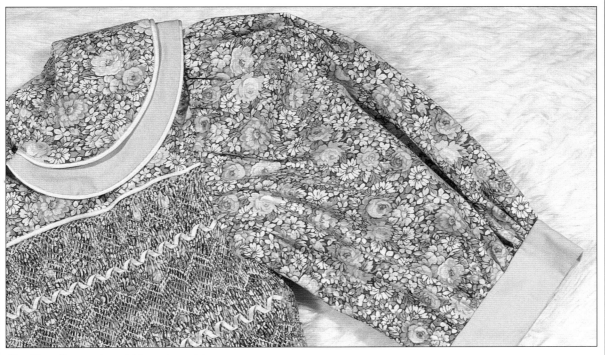

Double collar and matching sleeve trim

Nadia

This bright floral party dress in bold colours features short full sleeves trimmed with wide broderie anglaise and ribbon bows, and broderie anglaise collar and hem trim. The smocking is enhanced by the creative use of interwoven satin ribbon.

Instructions

Pleat 17 full-space rows.

Rows 1 and 17 are holding rows; do not smock.

Row 2: Work cable stitches across the row, then work a row of alternating cable.

Row 3: Work 3 cable stitches, then a baby wave up to row 2½ and back down to row 3. Work another 3 cable stitches, then another baby wave up to row 2½ and back down to row 3. Work another 3 cable stitches. Repeat the pattern across the row.

Rows 3½, 4 and 4½ are worked in the same pattern.

Row 5: Work baby waves down to row 5½, then back up to row 5. Continue to work zig-zag fashion, forming the top half of a diamond.

Row 6: Work baby waves up to row 5½ and then down to row 6. This forms the bottom half of the diamond. Make sure that the points meet. Ribbon can be woven through the diamonds after blocking.

Row 6½: Work 3 cable stitches along the row, then a baby wave down to row 7 and back up to row 6½. Work another 3 cable stitches, then a baby wave down to row 7. Repeat this pattern across the row.

Rows 7, 7½ and 8 are worked with the same stitch sequence.

Row 9: Work cable stitches along the row, then a row of alternating cable.

Row 10: Work 3 cable stitches, then a baby wave up to row 9½, and back down to row 10. Work another 3 cable stitches, then a baby wave up to row 9½. Repeat across the row.

Rows 10½, 11 and 11½ are worked with the same sequence of stitches.

Row 12: Work baby waves down to row 12½ then back up to row 12, forming a zig-zag.

Row 13: Work baby waves up to row 12½, then back down to row 13, forming the bottom half of the diamonds. Make sure that the points meet. Weave ribbon through the diamonds after blocking.

Row 13½: Work 3 cable stitches, than a baby wave down to row 14 and back up to row 13½. Work another 3 cable stitches, then a baby wave down to row 14. Continue with this sequence of stitches.

Rows 14, 14½ and 15 are worked in the same pattern.

Row 16: Work cable stitches along the row, then a row of alternating cable.

Row 1

Row 2

Row 3

Row 4

Row 5

Row 6

Row 7

Row 8

Row 9

Row 10

Row 11

Row 12

Row 13

Row 14

Row 15

Row 16

Row 17

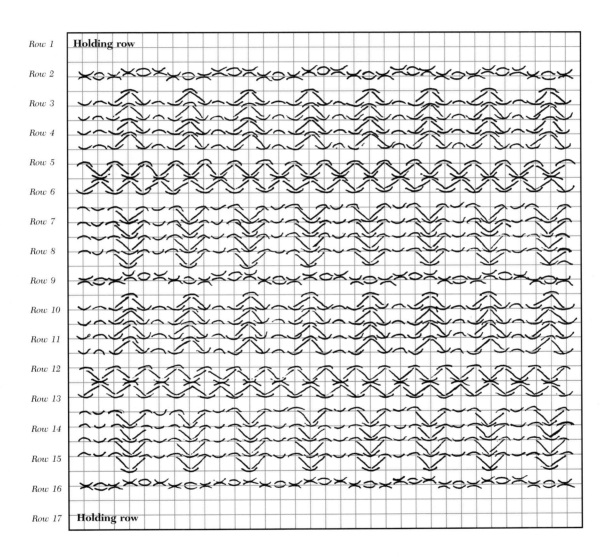

Nadia

Gloriously colourful fabric, smocking and ribbon weaving

Lavish use of broderie anglaise and fine ribbon

Primrose

_____

Reminiscent of a bygone era, this delightful bishop-style baby gown features delicate smocking around the neckline and sleeves with a hint of embroidery, and a matching smocked bonnet.

Instructions

Pleat 14 half-space rows.

Row 2: Work a row of cable stitches.
Row 3: Work a row of cable, then a row of alternating cable.
Row 5: Work a 2-step trellis up to row 4.
Row 6: Work a 2-step trellis up to row 5.
Row 7: Work a 2-step trellis up to row 6, then work row 7 down to row 9 with a 5-step trellis.
Row 8: Work a 5-step trellis down to row 10.
Row 9: Work a 5-step trellis down to row 11.
Row 11: Work a 5-step trellis down to row 13.
Row 13: Work a 5-step trellis up to row 11.

Three bullion roses have been embroidered in the three central hearts at the front of the garment.

Sleeves

Pleat 8 half-space rows.

Turn the sleeve upside down to work this design (starting with row 7).

Row 7: Work a row of cable stitches.
Row 5: Work row 5 up to row 4 and then down to row 6 with a baby wave.
Row 3: Work row 3 down to row 4 with a baby wave.

Find the centre front and mark this point with a pin. Work a 3-step trellis up to row 1 and down to row 3, on both sides of the pin mark. A bullion rose is embroidered at the pin mark.

Bonnet

Pleat 8 full-space rows.

Row 2: Work a row of cable stitches.
Row 3: Work a 3-step trellis down to row 4.
Row 4: Work a 3-step trellis down to row 5.
Row 5: Work a 3-step trellis down to row 6.
Row 7: Work a row of cable stitches.

DRESS

Row 1
Row 2
Row 3
Row 4
Row 5
Row 6
Row 7
Row 8
Row 9
Row 10
Row 11
Row 12
Row 13
Row 14

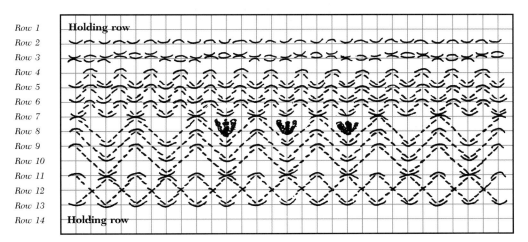

SLEEVE DETAIL

Row 1
Row 2
Row 3
Row 4
Row 5
Row 6
Row 7
Row 8

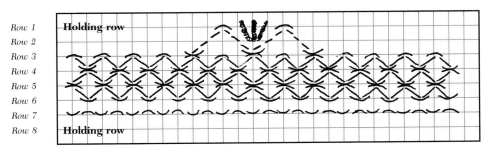

BONNET

Row 1
Row 2
Row 3
Row 4
Row 5
Row 6
Row 7
Row 8

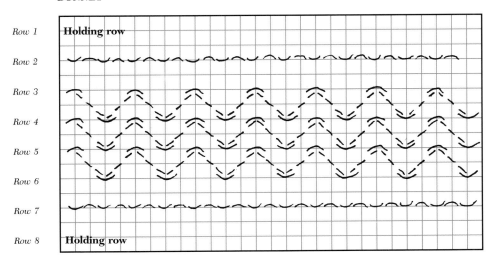

Primrose

Deep smocked circular yoke

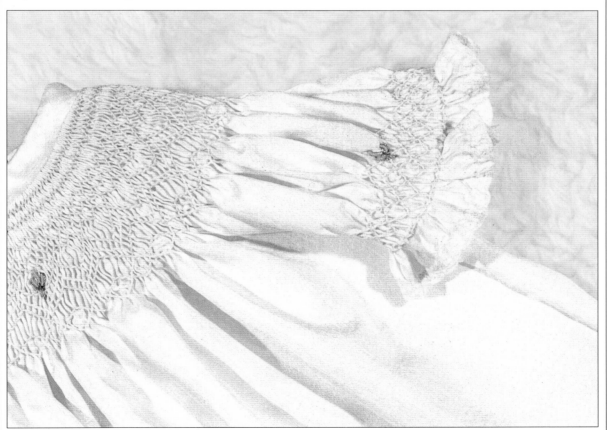

The sleeves are finished with bullion roses

Lucy

A striking effect is achieved with this bright floral fabric using a few simple smocking stitches (cables and baby waves), and highlighting with a pink satin ribbon. The short puff sleeves are trimmed with scolloped broderie anglaise and ribbon bows. The skirt features three deep tucks above the hem, which is trimmed with the same broderie anglaise used for the sleeves.

Instructions

Pleat 21 rows.

Row 2: Work cable stitches along row 2. Then starting directly below, work 5 cable stitches along row 2 and then a baby wave down to row 2½. Then work another 5 cable stitches back up to row 2, and a baby wave down to row 2½. Repeat this pattern.

Row 3: Using the same sequence of stitches, work row 3 with 5 cables then a baby wave up to row 2½, then work row 3 down to row 3½.

Row 4: Work row 4 up to row 3½, then down to row 4½.

Row 5: Work row 5 up to row 4½, then down to row 5½.

Row 6: Work row 6 up to row 5½. Starting directly under row 6 work a straight row of baby waves down to row 6½.

Row 7: Work row 7 up to row 6½, then row 7 down to row 7½.

Row 8: Work row 8 up to row 7½.

Ribbon can be woven through these rows of smocking if desired.

Row 8: Work 5 cables along row 8 and then a baby wave stitch down to row 8½, then back up to row 8 and work another 5 cable stitches.

Rows 2 to 8 are then repeated, down to row 20. (This design can easily be altered to any length required, for example repeat rows 2 to 13.)

Row 1   **Holding row**

Row 2

Row 3

Row 4

Row 5

Row 6

Row 7

Row 8

Row 9

Row 10

Row 11

Row 12

Row 13

Row 14

Row 15

Row 16

Row 17

Row 18

Row 19

Row 20

Row 21   **Holding row**

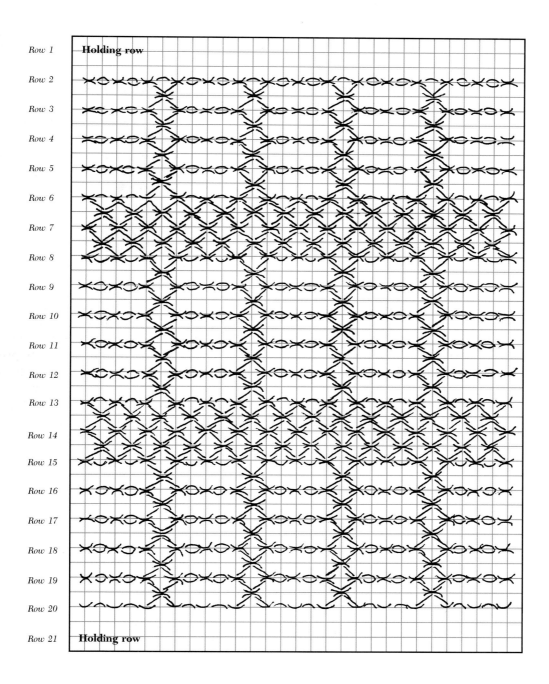

49

Lucy

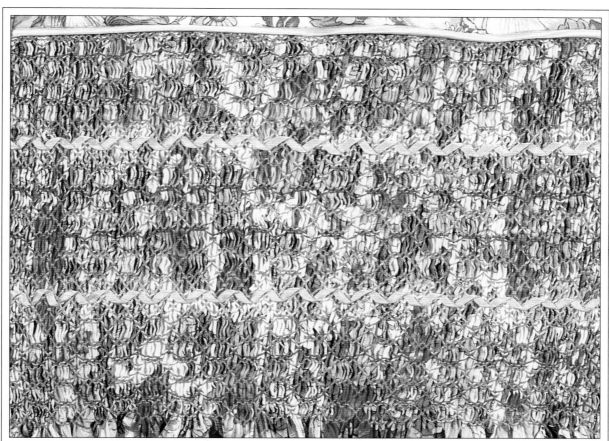

Deep smocked panel set off with ribbon weaving

Collar, sleeves and hem (see main picture) are trimmed with broderie anglaise

Vanessa

Traditional smocking sets off this attractive floral print. The dress has a piped collar and cream broderie anglaise on the hem and sleeve edges.

Instructions

Pleat 17 full-space rows.

Row 2: Work a row of cable stitches, starting with an under cable.
Row 3: Work a row of cable stitches starting with an under cable.

In between rows 2 and 3 count in 3 cable stitches and work 3 cables on the right side of the garment, push the needle to the back of the garment and work 3 cables, then bring the needle back through to the right side and work another 3 cables. Take the needle through to the wrong side again and repeat the design.

Row 4: Work row 4 down to row 5 with a 5-step trellis.
Row 5: Work row 5 up to row 4, and then down to row 6, with a 5-step trellis.
Row 6: Work row 6 up to row 5 with a 5-step trellis.

Work row 7 up to row 6, row 7½ up to row 6½, row 8 up to row 7, row 8½ up to row 7½, and row 9 up to row 8, all with a 5-step trellis.

If you have trouble judging the distance work rows 7, 8 and 9 first, then work the half-space rows in between.

Row 10: Work row 10 up to row 9 with a 5-step trellis, then down to row 9½ with a 2-step trellis, back up to row 9 with a 2-step trellis, and down to row 10 with a 5-step trellis. Repeat this pattern across the fabric. Starting again at row 10, repeat the design down to row 11 with a 5-step trellis, then up to row 10½ with a 2-step trellis, down to row 11 with a 2-step trellis, and back up to row 10 with a 5-step trellis, matching the pattern design as you work.

Rows 11, 11½, 12, 12½ and 13 are all worked with a 5-step trellis: row 11 down to row 12, row 11½ down to row 12½, row 12 down to row 13, row 12½ down to row 13½ and row 13 down to row 14. Work rows 11, 12 and 13 first, then work the half-space rows in between.

Row 14: Work row 14 down to row 15 with a 5-step trellis.
Row 15: Work row 15 up to row 14, then down to row 16, with a 5-step trellis.
Row 16: Work row 16 up to row 15 with a 5-step trellis.

Row 1   **Holding row**

Row 2

Row 3

Row 4

Row 5

Row 6

Row 7

Row 8

Row 9

Row 10

Row 11

Row 12

Row 13

Row 14

Row 15

Row 16

Row 17   **Holding row**

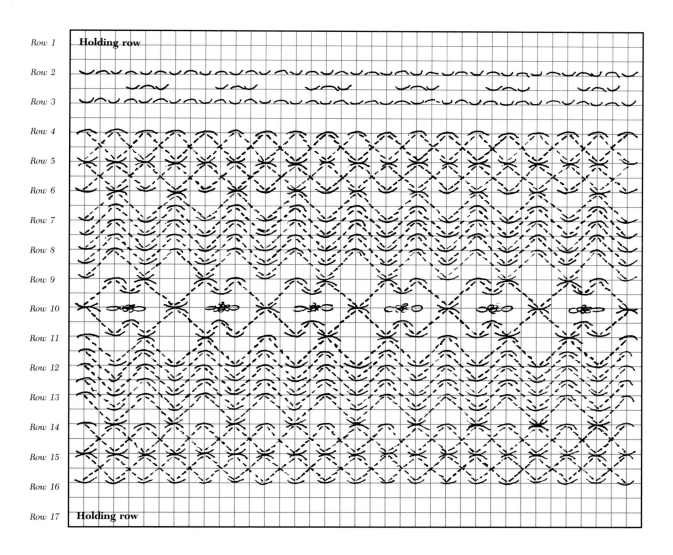

53

Vanessa

Soft colours used for the smocking allow the fabric pattern to show through

Hem is trimmed with a deep flounce of broderie anglaise

Jae's Christmas Dress

This classic garment in an unusual shade of jade green para silk features a delicately embroidered central diamond. Cream para silk is used for the piped collar and traditional cuffs. The main smocking consists of a 3-step trellis.

Instructions

Pleat 17 full-space rows.

Row 2: Row 2 is worked with a cable stitch, then a double cable directly underneath.

The following rows are all worked with a 3-step trellis.
Row 3: Work row 3 down to row 4.
Row 4: Up to row 3.
Row 5: Up to row 4, then down to row 6.
Row 6: Up to row 5.
Row 7: Up to row 6, then down to row 8.

Row 8: Up to row 7.
Row 9: Up to row 8, then down to row 10.
Row 10: Up to row 9.
Row 11: Up to row 10, then down to row 12.
Row 12: Up to row 11.
Row 13: Up to row 12, then down to row 14.
Row 14: Up to row 13.
Row 15: Up to row 14, then down to row 16.
Row 16: Up to row 15.

Embroidered diamond centre
Each side of the embroidered diamond is 6 small diamond shapes long. The embroidery consists of bullion roses, French knots, grub roses and lazy daisies.

Using the graphed design as a guide, mark the top point of the diamond, then the bottom. If you do not wish to use a marking pen or chalk use a coloured piece of thread. Then mark the points to the left and right. Embroider the flowers on trellis points as desired.

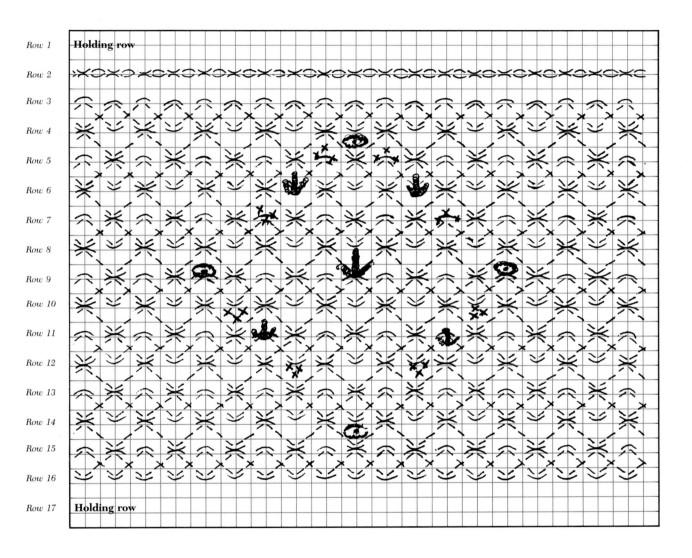

Row 1 — Holding row
Row 2
Row 3
Row 4
Row 5
Row 6
Row 7
Row 8
Row 9
Row 10
Row 11
Row 12
Row 13
Row 14
Row 15
Row 16
Row 17 — Holding row

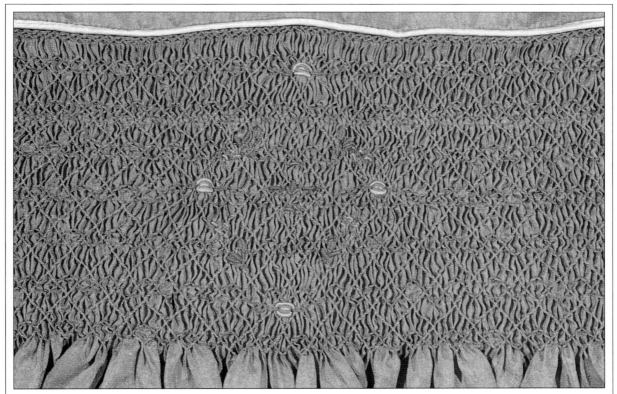

Embroidered diamond centre enhances smocked panel

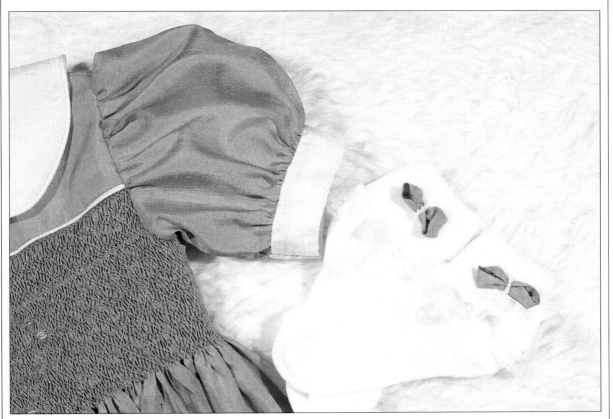

Piped collar and socks trimmed with bows of matching para silk

Somma

A captivating floral print with masses of tiny flowers in mauves, pinks, greens and apricots, smocked in traditional style with trellis stitches. The dress is trimmed with grub roses, wide broderie anglaise and pink satin piping.

Instructions

Pleat 24 full-space rows.

Row 2: Work a row of cable stitches.
Row 3: Work a row of cable stitches, then a row of alternating cable.
Row 4: Work row 4 down to row 5 with a 5-step trellis.
Row 5: Work row 5 up to row 4, then down to row 6, with a 5-step trellis.
Row 6: Work row 6 up to row 5, then down to row 7, with a 5-step trellis.
Row 7: Work row 7 up to row 6, then down to row 8, with a 5-step trellis.
Rows 8, 8½, 9, 9½, 10, 10½ and 11 are all worked with a 5-step trellis, starting downward. (I have used 4 different colours of thread.)

Centre of dress
Row 14: Work row 14 up to row 13 with a 5-step trellis, then down to row 13½ with a 2-step trellis, back up to row 13 with a 2-step trellis, and down to row 14 with a 5-step trellis. Work this pattern right across the fabric. Then work row 14 down to row 15 with a 5-step trellis, up to row 14½ with a 2-step trellis, back down to row 15 with 2-step trellis, and up to row 14 with a 5-step trellis. Make sure that all the cable points match up.

Now work rows 13½ and 14½ with the same pattern sequence, a half space distant.

Rows 16, 16½, 17, 17½, 18, 18½ and 19 are all smocked with a 5-step trellis starting downward.
Row 20: Work row 20 down to row 21 with a 5-step trellis.
Row 21: Work row 21 up to row 20, then down to row 22, with a 5-step trellis.
Row 22: Work row 22 up to row 21, then down to row 23, with a 5-step trellis.
Row 23: Work row 23 up to row 22 with a 5-step trellis. (Rows 20 to 23 cross over each other, so try using different coloured threads.)

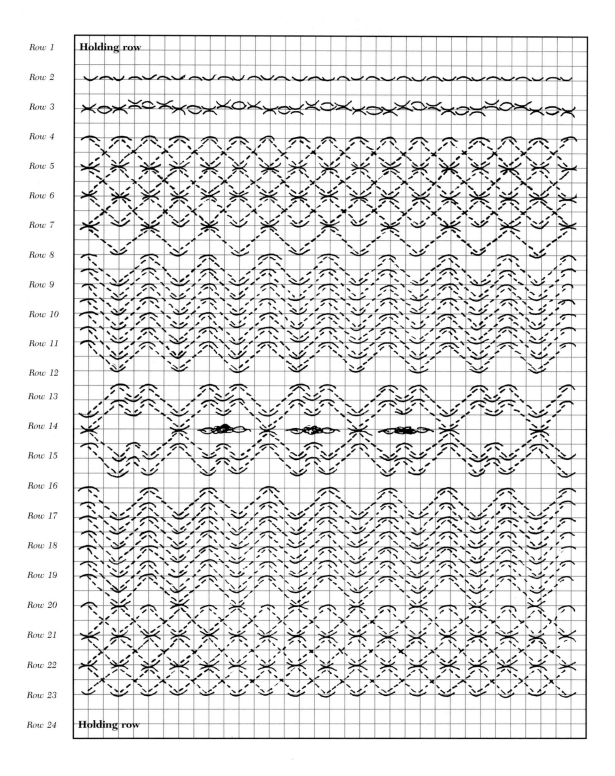

Row 1
Row 2
Row 3
Row 4
Row 5
Row 6
Row 7
Row 8
Row 9
Row 10
Row 11
Row 12
Row 13
Row 14
Row 15
Row 16
Row 17
Row 18
Row 19
Row 20
Row 21
Row 22
Row 23
Row 24

61

Somma

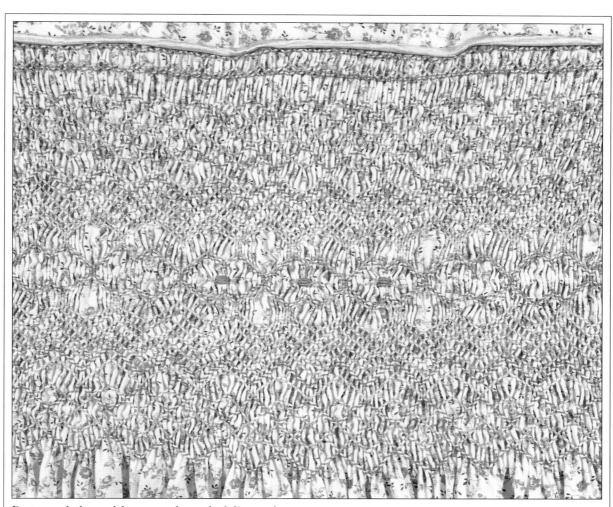

Deep smocked panel has central panel of diamonds

Callen's Christening Robe

A delightful bishop-style christening gown with smocked sleeves.

Tiny pearl buttons surrounded by bullion flowers and ribbon bows with layers of tucks and lace will make this gown an heirloom.

Instructions

Pleat 11 half-space rows.

Row 2: Work a row of cable stitches.
Row 3: Work another row of cable stitches.
Row 4: Work 3 cable stitches, then a wave stitch down to row 5, then work another 3 cable stitches, and a wave stitch back up to row 4. Repeat this pattern across the row.

Repeat the sequence through to row 10, following the design graph.

Sleeve detail
Pleat 7 half-space rows.

Row 2: Work a row of cable stitches along the row.
Row 4: Starting at row 4 work 3 cable stitches, bring the needle up to row 3 and work another 3 cable stitches, then down to row 4 and work another 3 cable stitches. Starting directly underneath row 4 work 3 cable stitches along, then down to row 5 and work another 3 cable stitches.
Row 6: Work cable stitches along the row.

Tucks and pintucks
After sewing up the gown, use the guide to mark where tucks, lace and pintucks are required. Press the tucks firmly and sew lace under them where desired; then sew in each tuck. Sew in the pintucks, and lastly position the pearl buttons and tack them into place. Work bullion roses around each pearl button and secure the button in place. Make tiny bows and sew firmly in position.

TUCK GUIDE

Tuck

Lace

Tuck

Tuck

Pintuck

Pintuck

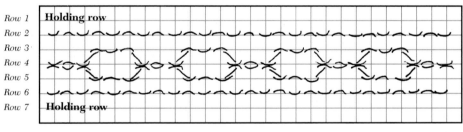

Pintuck

Pintuck

Tuck

Tuck

Tuck

Tuck

Tuck

Lace

ROBE AND BONNET

Row 1 **Holding row**
Row 2
Row 3
Row 4
Row 5
Row 6
Row 7
Row 8
Row 9
Row 10
Row 11 **Holding row**

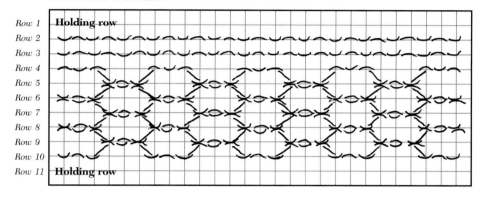

SLEEVE DETAIL

Row 1 **Holding row**
Row 2
Row 3
Row 4
Row 5
Row 6
Row 7 **Holding row**

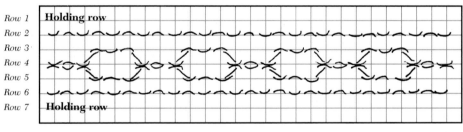

65

Callen

Simple circular bonnet with smocked trim

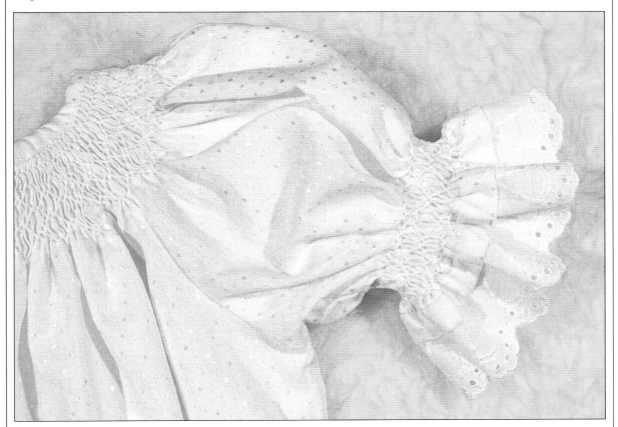

Detail of sleeve and neckline of christening robe

Melinda

This charming floral dress is smocked with soft mauves, dusky pinks and muted greens in a simple 4-step trellis, all worked in the same direction. Although 19 full-space rows are pleated, the half-space rows are also worked, allowing plenty of scope for colour combinations.

The contrasting cuffs are covered with crocheted cotton lace.

Instructions

Pleat 19 full-space rows.

Row 2: Work row 2 with cable stitch, then with alternating cable stitches.

Row 3½ up to row 2½.

Row 4 up to row 3.

Row 4½ up to row 3½.

Row 5 up to row 4.

Row 5½ up to row 4½.

Row 6 up to row 5.

Continue this pattern through to row 18.

Change thread colour as desired. Two rows of smocking worked in the same colour are most attractive. For example, rows 4 and 4½ in dusky pink, rows 5 and 5½ in muted green, and rows 6 and 6½ in a soft mauve.

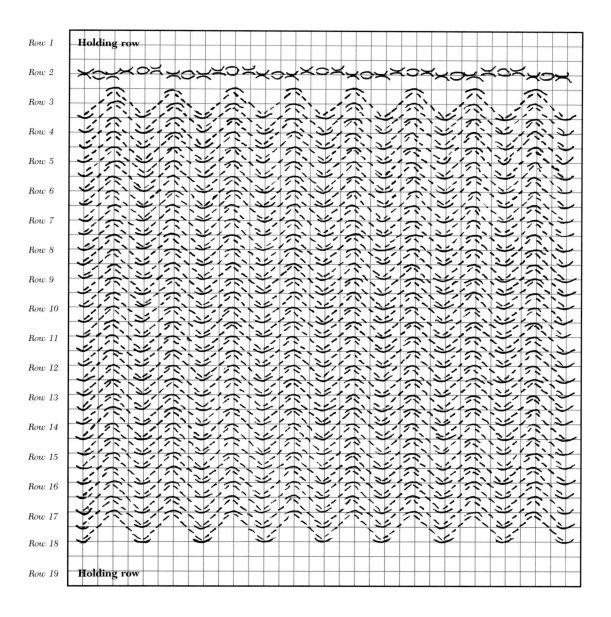

Row 1   **Holding row**

Row 2

Row 3

Row 4

Row 5

Row 6

Row 7

Row 8

Row 9

Row 10

Row 11

Row 12

Row 13

Row 14

Row 15

Row 16

Row 17

Row 18

Row 19   **Holding row**

Melinda

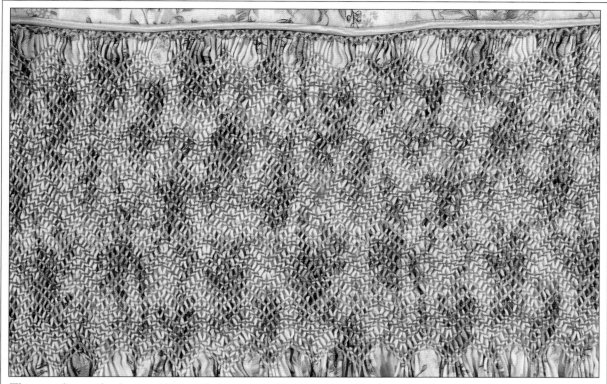

The use of several colours adds complexity to an allover 4-step trellis design

Collar and smocked panel are trimmed with satin piping, and the cuffs with cotton lace

Lana

This dress has an old-fashioned Victorian look. The muted tones are enhanced by the plain contrast fabric used as a trim to attach the front yoke to the front bodice, and for the cuff edges and collar. A deep tuck inserted above the hem is in the same fabric.

Instructions

Pleat 18 full-space rows.

Row 2: Row 2 is worked with cable stitches.

Row 3: Row 3 is worked with a row of cable stitches, then with a row of alternating cable.

Row 4: Work row 4 down to row 5 with a 5-step trellis.

Row 5: Work row 5 up to row 4 with a 5-step trellis, and then down to row 6 with a 5-step trellis.

Row 6: Work row 6 up to row 5 with a 5-step trellis.

Row 7: Work row 7 up to row 6 with a 5-step trellis.

Row 8: Work row 8 up to row 7 with a 5-step trellis.

Now work row 8 down to row 8½ with a 2-step trellis, then back up to row 8 with a 2-step trellis, then down to row 9 with a 5-step trellis, and back up to row 8 with a 5-step trellis. Repeat the pattern sequence across the row.

Rows 9 and 9½ are worked with the same trellis pattern sequence.

Row 12: Work row 12 with a two-step trellis up to row 11½, then down to row 12 with a 2-step trellis, then a 5-step trellis up to row 11, and back down to row 12 with a 5-step trellis.

Rows 12½ and 13 are worked with the same trellis pattern sequence, making sure that the pattern corresponds to rows 8, 8½ and 9. Bullion roses have been worked in the centre (between rows 10 and 11). Back smock rows 10 and 11.

Row 13: Work row 13 down to row 14 with a 5-step trellis.

Row 14: Work row 14 down to row 15 with a 5-step trellis.

Row 15: Work row 15 down to row 16 with a 5-step trellis.

Row 16: Work row 16 up to row 15 with a 5-step trellis, then work row 16 down to row 17 with a 5-step trellis.

Row 17: Work row 17 up to row 16 with a 5-step trellis.

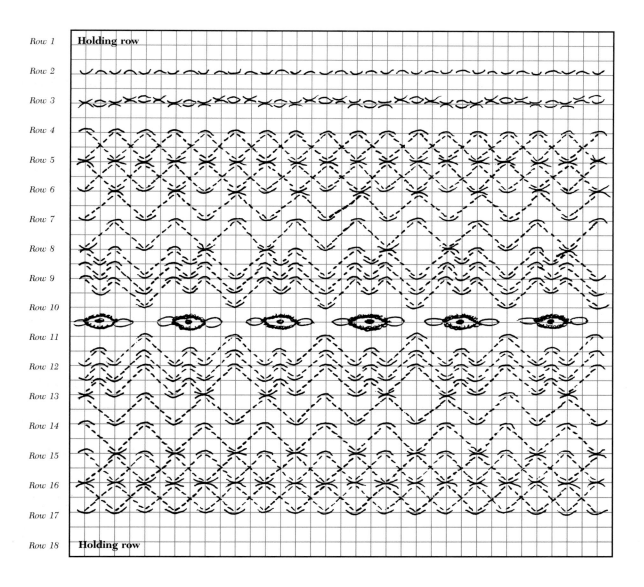

Row 1   **Holding row**

Row 2

Row 3

Row 4

Row 5

Row 6

Row 7

Row 8

Row 9

Row 10

Row 11

Row 12

Row 13

Row 14

Row 15

Row 16

Row 17

Row 18   **Holding row**

Lana

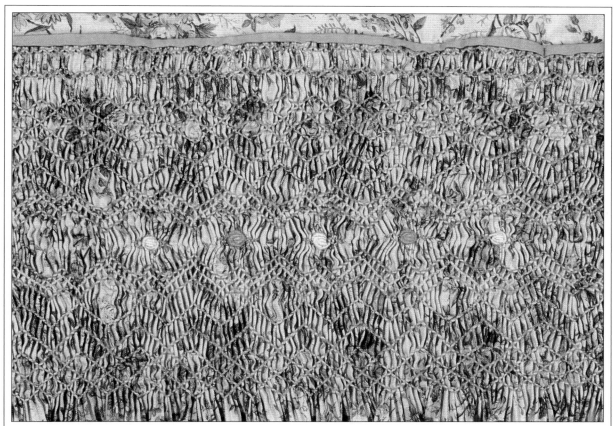

Smocked panel has bullion rose embroidery

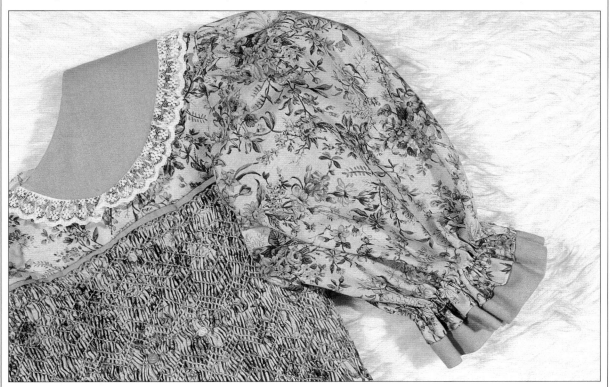

Collar and sleeve details

Rhapsody Blue

A crisp white collar and cuffs with gathered cotton lace edging bring out the colours in this traditional smocked garment.

Instructions: Pleat 23 half-space rows.

Row 2: Work cable stitches across the row, then work a row of alternating cable.

Row 4: Starting at row 4 with an under cable, bring the needle up to row 3 and work 3 cable stitches along row 3, then a baby wave down to row 4. Bring the needle back up to row 3 and work 3 cable stitches along the row, then another baby wave down to row 4. Repeat the pattern to the end of the row.

Row 3: Work row 3 with an above cable first, then bring the needle down to row 4 and work 3 cable stitches along the row, then work a baby wave up to row 3.

This is a 3-cable and 1 baby wave cross-over combination, using 2 contrasting colours.

Row 6: Begin row 6 with an under cable, bring the needle up to row 5 and work 3 cable stitches, then take the needle down to row 6 and work a baby wave stitch. Take the needle back up to row 5 and work 3 more cable stitches, then one baby wave down to row 6. Repeat the pattern across the row.

Row 7: Row 7 is worked in the same direction as row 6, with a 3 cable and 1 baby wave combination.

Now reverse the combination starting at row 7 and work the 3 cables along row 8, bringing the needle up to row 7 for a baby wave. Then work row 8 down to row 9, repeating the previous pattern (see the design graph).

Rows 10 and 11 are worked the same as rows 3 and 4.

Row 12: Work a cable row, then an alternating cable.

Rows 13 and 14 are the same as rows 3 and 4.

Rows 16 up to 15, 17 up to 16, 17 down to 18, and 18 down to 19 are worked the same as rows 6 to 8. Follow the design graph.

Rows 20 and 21 are worked the same as rows 3 and 4.

Row 22: Work a cable row, then an alternating cable.

Row 1
Row 2
Row 3
Row 4
Row 5
Row 6
Row 7
Row 8
Row 9
Row 10
Row 11
Row 12
Row 13
Row 14
Row 15
Row 16
Row 17
Row 18
Row 19
Row 20
Row 21
Row 22
Row 23

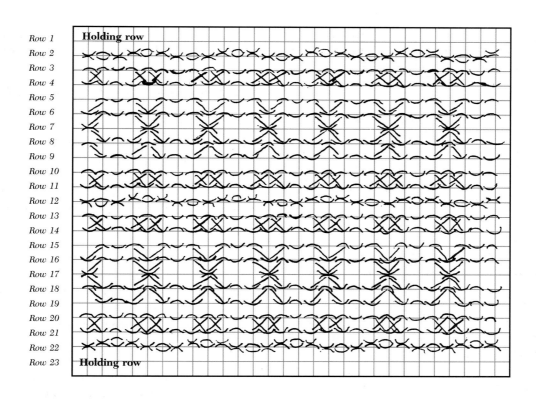

Rhapsody Blue

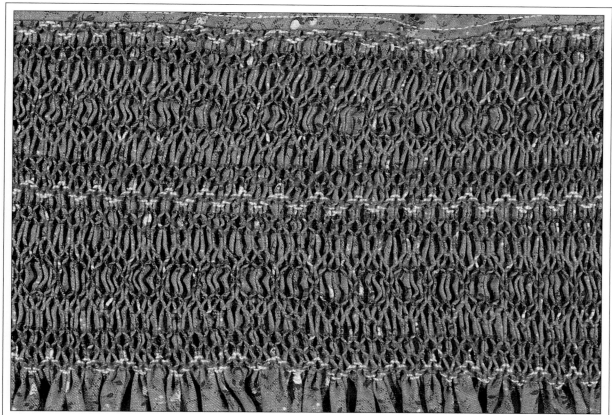

Detail of smocked panel

Sleeve and collar are trimmed with broderie anglaise

79

Index

Mathematics
for **Key Stage Three**

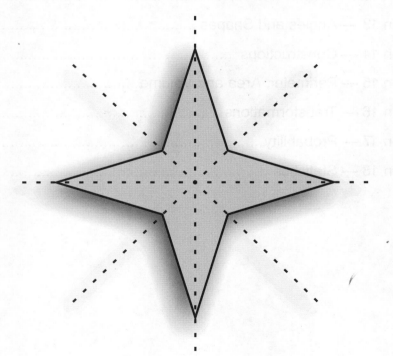

Answers for **Book One**

Mathematics for **Key Stage Three**

Contents

Published by CGP

ISBN: 978 1 78294 165 1
www.cgpbooks.co.uk

Printed by Elanders Ltd, Newcastle upon Tyne.